THE KINGDOM HAS DRAWN NEAR
STUDIES IN THE GOSPEL JESUS PREACHED

THE KINGDOM
HAS DRAWN NEAR

Studies in the Gospel Jesus Preached

Benjamin W. Miller

Sensus Divinitatis Publishing

New York

The Kingdom Has Drawn Near:
Studies in the Gospel Jesus Preached
ISBN 978-0-578-02047-1
Copyright © 2009 Benjamin W. Miller
All rights reserved.

First published in May 2009 by Sensus Divinitatis Publishing.

For current information about all releases from
Sensus Divinitatis Publishing, please visit our website:
www.sensusdivinitatis.com

I wish to dedicate this work to my wife, Sarah, who, in the microcosmic domain of our home, and as a helper suitable in my pastoral ministry, is to me an unspeakably precious "fellow worker for the kingdom of God."

The following studies were originally four sermons preached on consecutive Sunday mornings in August 2008, at the Orthodox Presbyterian Church in Franklin Square, New York. Except where the author has provided his own translation or paraphrase, Scripture quotations are taken from the English Standard Version (ESV).

TABLE OF CONTENTS

In writing these essays, and in preaching the sermons upon which they are based, I have felt myself always at the margins of my subject. Confronted with the depth, the vastness, the sheer grandeur of the story, idea, and reality that is the kingdom of God, I have tried to scribble a few marginal notes, some brief sketches of what I have seen and heard. The gospel of the kingdom – the gospel Jesus Christ preached – is, in a true sense, the story of everything. It is, in my view (though others have said so before me, and said it better), the central theme of Holy Scripture, the basic reality and explanation of the cosmos, and the cornerstone of Reformed theology (to which tradition I happily, thankfully belong).

The 21st century is witnessing something of a resurgence of what is called "Calvinism," or "the Reformed faith." Central to this resurgence is a revival of the biblical notion that God is *sovereign* in the salvation of sinners; that God by free and irresistible grace takes sinners dead in sins and trespasses and grants them full pardon, spiritual life, the seed of all graces, and eternal glory in his presence. What is not always remembered in the midst of this resurgence is that historical Calvinism, or Reformation theology, following Scripture, did not view God's sovereignty as operative only in the soteriological sphere, the sphere of saving sinners. Reformation theology, listening to Scripture, understood that God is sovereign over *all* of human life and indeed over *all* created things in heaven and on earth. His law is the unchallengeable rule of human ethics, the supreme standard to which every human institution is accountable; his will governs every event of history, and will in time usher in a new heavens and a new earth wherein righteousness dwells, and from which all sin and all sinners are permanently removed.

In his famous Stone Lectures at Princeton University in 1898, Abraham Kuyper said the root principle or dominating principle of Calvinism is "not, soteriologically, justification by faith, but, in the widest sense cosmologically, *the Sovereignty of the Triune God over the whole Cosmos*, in all its spheres and kingdoms, visible and invisible."[1] We might put it slightly differently: the dominant theme, the metanarrative of Calvinism, or Reformed theology, is the kingdom of

God. Unless this dominant theme is recovered in all of its fullness, the Calvinism of the 21st century will be but a shadow of its former self, because it is less than fully biblical. If the essays that follow aid in that recovery, I shall be more than rewarded for the small pains expended in writing them.

Benjamin W. Miller
February 2009

CHAPTER ONE

THE KINGDOM
AND THE COVENANT

Scripture Readings:

Isaiah 9:2–7

Mark 1:14–15

INTRODUCTION

I find myself perennially fascinated by the shaping power of ideas. Everyone has ideas. I have ideas. You have ideas. I don't know all of your ideas; perhaps that's just as well. I'm certainly glad you don't know all of mine; but everyone has them. Everyone has thoughts. Everyone has perceptions and opinions and plans and so on. And everyone who has ideas (which is all of us) lives according to those ideas. What you choose to watch on a television program at night depends on your ideas about a great many things. Whether you decide to fly a plane into the World Trade Center depends on your ideas. There are different kinds of ideas, and they shape us in different ways.

There are ideas that expand the soul. There are ideas that shrink and shrivel souls. There are ideas that nourish the soul, and there are ideas that starve the soul. I happen to like soda crackers in my soup, but if I were to diet every day on nothing but soda crackers, I would proceed very quickly to a state of emaciation, then to starvation, then to a long and very thin wooden box. This makes perfect sense to us in the realm of the body, but it is true as well in the realm of the soul. It is sad to me when I meet people (and one meets them often) who have dieted so long on small, silly ideas that they have either lost, or they have never even developed the capacity for, great ideas that expand and nourish the soul. There are ideas that can inspire, that can win the heart, that can capture the imagination, that can stir to noble action; and there are ideas that weaken and numb and deaden the soul of man.

The Bible is a book that overflows with great ideas, and that is actually a nearly irreverent statement. These are not *great* ideas. These are the *greatest* ideas, because they are the ideas of God himself. The Bible is not, over against so much popular thinking today, a book for religious "kooks" who have forgotten how to think. The Bible is *the* book that opens up to us the unbounded, inexhaustible thought-world of God himself. The Bible opens up to us the ideas, the plans, the purposes – what the Bible calls the very wisdom – of God. To live in this universe, to feed on these ideas of God himself, is to find the Tree of Life. The father writing to his son in Proverbs 3 says, "My son . . . blessed is the one who finds wisdom . . . . She is a tree of life to those who lay hold of her; those who hold her fast are called blessed" (Proverbs 3:13, 18). He who finds the wisdom of God finds the Tree of Life.

What I want to explore with you in this and the following three studies is an idea and a reality that lies at the very center of the Scriptures. Suppose someone were to say to you, "You Christians are always talking about the Bible, the ideas of God in the Bible. What is the central idea of the Bible? What are the central ideas of the Bible?" I wonder how you might answer that question. I wonder how many of us would immediately think of the answer that will be proposed in these four studies.

I want to suggest and try to persuade you as best I can by the help of the Holy Spirit that at the very center of the thought-world of God himself is an idea (and a reality!) called *the kingdom of God*. No less a luminary than Herman Bavinck, the great theologian of the last century, said this: "The essence of the Christian religion . . . ." Let us pause a moment. Suppose you were asked, "What is the essence of the Christian religion? What are you Christians all about? What distinguishes you?" What would you say? "The essence of the Christian religion," says Bavinck, "consists in the reality that the creation of the Father, ruined by sin, is restored in the death of the Son of God and re-created by the grace of the Holy Spirit into a kingdom of God."[2] This is a glorious definition. The sheer trinitarianism of it is glorious – that all three Persons of the Godhead are at work here. And notice that the end and goal of all their working is a *kingdom*, the kingdom of God. What do you think of this?

Perhaps you don't believe it, or perhaps you don't even like it. Maybe you are saying to yourself, "When I read the Bible, I don't see the kingdom of God as particularly central; in fact, I see other things as much more central." Perhaps talk of the centrality of the kingdom sounds as if it is drifting away from the centrality of Jesus' work in saving sinners, away from the centrality of redemption over into a kind of social gospel that is interested simply in seeing society transformed. Isn't the center of the Bible the cross and resurrection of Jesus Christ? Or maybe the idea of the kingdom of God makes you nervous for other reasons. Perhaps it is linked in your mind with a kind of unsavory Christian triumphalism, a pridefulness and desire to dominate that masquerades as Christianity (of which the world has seen far too much). These are legitimate concerns, and we will need to address them in what follows.

Let us begin, then, with the teachings of Jesus of Nazareth; we cannot do better than to begin where our Lord himself begins. Notice in our text, Mark 1:14–15, the place that Jesus, the founder of our religion, gives to the kingdom of God. We will open up the text using two questions: (1) What does Jesus say is the *precise content* of the "gospel," the "good news"? (2) What does he say is the *proper response* to the gospel?

WHAT DOES JESUS SAY IS THE PRECISE CONTENT OF THE GOSPEL?

First of all, what in these verses does Jesus tell us is the precise content of the gospel? It is very interesting that Jesus announces the "good news" of God in these terms. He is preaching, we are told, proclaiming the good news (that's what "gospel" means), the glad tidings of the *kingdom of God*. This is what Jesus says: "The time has been fulfilled, and the kingdom of God has drawn near. Turn; repent, and believe in the good news. Believe in the glad tidings." That is how Jesus announces the gospel.

What is interesting is that he does not give us here any definition of the kingdom of God. He seems to assume that his hearers will know what he is talking about. What is the kingdom of God? We are given some help in the phrase, "The time has been fulfilled [for the kingdom to draw near]." One gets the sense that a long period of time has elapsed and has now come to an expected moment of fulfillment. The idea of the arrival of the kingdom must have a very long history. This must be a reality that has been anticipated for quite some time; which leads us to believe that the explanation, the definition we are looking for, lies in the Scriptures of what we call the Old Testament or Old Covenant,[3] or what the New Testament writers frequently refer to as "the law and the prophets."

We may recall in light of this that Jesus says in Luke 16:16, "The law and the prophets were until John [the Baptizer]; since then the good news of the kingdom of God is preached." We find here in Mark 1:14 that John has been put in prison. The last of the Old

Testament prophets, the final representative of "the law and the prophets," has been silenced as the time of prophecy is giving way to the time of fulfillment. We need, then, to turn back to the law and the prophets and ask how the kingdom of God was conceived, envisioned, and anticipated in those Old Covenant Scriptures.

THE OLD COVENANT HOPE
OF THE KINGDOM OF GOD

Let us take a few moments to walk through the biblical record of the Old Covenant hope of the kingdom of God. What do the law and the prophets tell us about the coming kingdom of God? We can narrate this as something of a story (which it is!).

Once upon a time, in the beginning, Yahweh, the Lord God of heaven and earth, ruled the entire cosmos. According to Psalm 47:2, he is a great king, *the* great king over all the earth, and he has been such since he made the world. The earth and all that it contains, all of creation, was and is the kingdom of Yahweh.

Adam, in the beginning, was God's representative king and God's representative priest on earth. As king, he was to take dominion over all creation. God said, "Let us make man in our image . . . and let them [male and female] have dominion over [all created things]" (Genesis 1:26). Adam was to represent the lordship of Yahweh God by ruling and governing and shaping the environment God had given him there in Eden and beyond. He was also to be a priest; he was to gather all of creation in the worship of the Great King, and he was to purge out of Eden anything that might defile Yahweh's sanctuary. He made a fairly miserable job of it, as we shall see.

Eden, then, – this garden kingdom – was to be a place of *dominion* and *communion*, a place where Adam ruled for God and communed with God. But when Adam (you know the story well) joined with Satan in rebelling against Yahweh, his dominion and communion were substantially disrupted. God cursed the ground, and no longer would it yield under Adam's dominion as it once had; it would bring forth instead rebellious thorns and thistles. And his communion with God was disrupted, as God ejected him and his wife out of the garden to wander in the earth.

But in this dark moment, you will remember, Yahweh interposed; while cursing the serpent, he announced that there was a line of the human seed to come from the woman over which he would rule in *grace*. "I will put enmity," he said to Satan, "between your seed and the seed of the woman." From this line of the woman's seed, he told the serpent, there would come One through whom God's creation kingdom will be fully restored. The image of the heel of this One-to-come crushing the head of the serpent (Genesis 3:15) is a metaphor that tells us every influence of Satan will in time be eradicated. It is a wonderful promise, what we call the first gospel promise.

It is striking that, as the story of humankind begins to unfold from this point forward in the book of Genesis, we find humankind straightway beginning efforts to recover their dominion and their communion. Cain went out from the presence of the Lord and built a city (Genesis 4:17). A "city" is a place where man seeks to establish dominion over a piece of ground. Think of Manhattan: the building of this city is an exercise of dominion, taking a relatively tiny piece of real estate and erecting a kind of kingdom on it – ruling it, subduing it, making it a place that flourishes and is full of a kind of glory. This Cain immediately sought to do.

Equally striking is the language when the sons of men begin to build the tower of Babel. Humankind is lonely, alienated, scattered, cursed. Notice what they intend when they begin building the city in Genesis 11:4. They say, "Come, let us build ourselves a city and a tower with its top in the heavens." And notice: "Let us make a name for ourselves [make ourselves lords once again] lest we be dispersed over the face of the whole earth" – scattered abroad in ignominy; all communion, all sense of community, fellowship, and togetherness shattered as we are scattered throughout the earth. Humankind is grasping again at dominion and communion. Their efforts, you will recall, are decisively thwarted by Yahweh, who then brings forward the blueprints of his own kingdom-building work in what we call the covenant promises to Abraham.

In Genesis 12, in God's covenant promises to Abraham, we find language that parallels the earlier account of the tower of Babel. He says to Abraham in Genesis 12:2, "I will make of you a great nation." Here is the reality of which Babel was the counterfeit. A "great nation": the idea of *kingdom* lies at the very heart and center of the Abrahamic promises! "I will make of you, Abram [that was his name at the time], a great nation. I will bless you and make your name great, so that you will be a blessing. I will bless those who bless you, and him who dishonors you I will curse, and in you all the families of the earth shall be blessed" (Genesis 12:2–3).

This is one "bookend" of Abraham's life. We then turn to Genesis 22, the other bookend of his life, and note what God says just after the incident on Mount Moriah in which Abraham was asked to sacrifice Isaac his son. God says in Genesis 22:17–18 (rendered literally), "Blessing I will bless you, and multiplying I will multiply your offspring as the stars of the heaven and as the sand that is on the seashore." And observe the kingdom language: "Your offspring, Abraham, shall possess the gate of his enemies, and in your offspring shall all the nations of the earth be blessed, because you have obeyed my voice." In your seed, Abraham, says God, I will build a kingdom in which blessing and communion with me are fully restored. I will make of you a kingdom that possesses, that takes dominion over, the gate of its enemies; and that kingdom will include nothing less than all the families of the earth.

All of these kingdom-promises made to Abraham become explicit by the end of what we call the patriarchal period. We trace the stories of Abraham, Isaac, Jacob, and Jacob's twelve sons, until we come to Genesis 49. Now we are at the other end of the period of Israel's fathers, on the threshold of the time in Egypt after which God will deliver Israel through Moses in the Exodus. The line of promise has narrowed over this long period from Abraham to Isaac, his son; then to Jacob, Isaac's son; then to Judah, Jacob's son.

Nowhere in Genesis is the kingdom concept more explicit than in the prophecy Jacob delivers over Judah in Genesis 49. The old patriarch says, "Judah, your brothers shall praise you; your hand shall be on the neck of your enemies; your father's sons shall bow down before you. Judah is a lion's cub; from the prey, my son, you have gone up. He stooped down; he crouched as a lion and as a lioness; who dares rouse him? The scepter shall not depart from Judah, nor the ruler's staff from between his feet, until Shiloh comes [this being a reference to the coming of the Messiah]; and to him shall be the obedience of the peoples" (Genesis 49:8–10).

And what kind of a kingdom will be in those days? Grape vines, says Jacob, will be so common that they will be used for hitching posts.[4] "Binding his foal to the vine and his donkey's colt to the choice vine, he has washed his garments in wine and his vesture in the blood of grapes." Wine will be like wash water, there will be so much of it! "His eyes are darker than wine, and his teeth whiter than milk" (Genesis 49:11–12). It will be a time of astonishing prosperity and blessedness in this kingdom when "Shiloh comes."

As you think about the storyline of the Old Testament, you will remember that these promises to Abraham and his sons were initially fulfilled in the kingdom God established at Mount Sinai. In connection with this, look at one verse at the end of Deuteronomy. Now we are jumping far ahead to the end of what we call the Pentateuch, the first five books of the Bible. At the very end of Moses' life, as he gives his final blessing before he dies and Joshua takes command, he remembers back to Mount Sinai: "The Lord came from Sinai and dawned from Seir upon us; he shone forth from Mount Paran" (Deuteronomy 33:2). Then a few verses later: "Moses commanded us a law [he is thinking back to the scene at Mount Sinai], as a possession for the assembly of Jacob." Now notice the language: "Thus the LORD [Yahweh] became king in Jeshurun [a name for Israel]" (Deuteronomy 33:4–5).

When the leaders of the people were gathered, all the tribes of Israel together, Yahweh became *king* over this nation on that day. On that day, Yahweh ruled over a willing people, a people who said, "All that the LORD has spoken we will do" (Exodus 19:8). And God said to them that day, "If you will keep my covenant . . . you shall be to me a kingdom of priests and a holy nation" (Exodus 19:5–6). In effect God was saying, "*You shall be to me what Adam was.* You shall be to me kings over the land of Canaan. You shall be my priests who are also my kings, who will enjoy communion with me, access into my very presence in my land." God brings them into his place, into his land, a land that flows with milk and honey, a land that is a kind of Eden restored. And he sets up over them there the dynasty of the tribe of Judah, as promised in Genesis 49.

Here we jump ahead again. Under Solomon, David's greatest son, the dominion of God's kingdom in Israel extended to the ends of the earth. We think of the prophetic prayer in Psalm 72, titled "A Psalm of Solomon." Whether Solomon wrote it or David wrote it *about* Solomon is neither immediately clear nor our concern here, but the language about the Solomonic kingdom is highly significant: "May he [the king] have dominion from sea to sea, and from the River [Euphrates] to the ends of the earth!" We sing of this in the great hymn: "His large and great dominion shall from sea to sea extend; it from the River shall reach forth to earth's remotest end. Yea, kings shall all before him bow, all nations shall obey . . . ." Those who dwell in the wilderness will bow down before the king, says the psalmist, "and his enemies lick the dust! May the kings of Tarshish and of the coastlands render him tribute; may the kings of Sheba and Seba bring gifts! May all kings fall down before him, all nations serve him" (Psalm 72:8–11).

In fact, this is just what occurred (1 Kings 4:24–25). Solomon's kingdom spread so far that the Queen of Sheba brought gifts, seeking his wisdom. Not only the *dominion* of his kingdom spread to the world's end; also in his days the *communion* of God with his people, that other component of God's kingdom on earth, was permanently established in the beautiful temple Solomon built. This glorious structure stood as a kind of microcosm of God's reestablished kingdom on a renewed and flourishing earth.

These are cheerful, delightful, beautiful, enjoyable things to read about, but . . . and there is always a "but" in the Old Testament. In the end, Israel and her kings proved to be no more obedient than Adam, and they lost their dominion, and their place of communion was destroyed as the Babylonian hordes razed Solomon's temple. Israel was thrown out of Canaan and scattered to the ends of the earth, just as Adam was thrown out of Eden, and just as Adam's descendants were scattered to the ends of the earth after their attempt to build the tower at Babel.

In this dark period, when it appeared that God's kingdom-building work had failed, the prophets began to envision a new kingdom age, over which would rule a Child whose righteousness, as we read in Isaiah 9:7, would never fail. And how could it fail, for this

Child would be God himself? He would be Wonderful. He would be the Counselor, the Mighty God, the Everlasting Father, the Prince of peace. *God in this coming age would take the kingdom into his own hands.*

We jump ahead one last time. In the prophecies of Daniel, a timeline was given for the arrival of this new kingdom age. At the end of Daniel's prophecy to Nebuchadnezzar regarding the image of gold (Daniel 2:31–45), the four parts of the image were said to represent four great Gentile empires about to arise, of which Nebuchadnezzar was the first. The mighty Babylonian empire ruled by Nebuchadnezzar was, in fact, followed by the Medo-Persian empire, then the Greek empire, and finally the Roman empire.

At the very end of the prophecy (Daniel 2:44), God told Nebuchadnezzar through Daniel that "in the days of these kings," in the days of Gentile world-domination, the God of heaven would set up a kingdom "that shall never be destroyed, nor shall the kingdom be left to another people. It shall break in pieces all these kingdoms and bring them to an end, and it shall stand forever." God, in the days of Gentile world-domination, would set up a kingdom that would destroy all others and fill the entire earth (Daniel 2:35).

Thus something of a timeline was set for the arrival of the Old Covenant hope of the kingdom of God.

THE NEW COVENANT ANNOUNCEMENT
OF THE KINGDOM OF GOD

Having observed, in broad strokes, what the law and the prophets said about the coming of God's kingdom on earth, we return to the pages of the New Testament, and in the very opening lines we find God everywhere announcing the arrival of his kingdom! After four hundred years of silence, God is speaking again, and picking up right where he left off, he speaks about the kingdom.

Take, for instance, the first chapter of Luke's gospel. Can you imagine what it must have been like for a young girl named Mary to hear these words: "Do not be afraid, Mary, for you have found favor with God. And behold, you will conceive in your womb and bear a son, and you shall call his name Jesus"? Perhaps thus far you see nothing particularly radical here. But then: "He will be great and will be called the Son of the Most High. And the Lord God will give to him the throne of his father David, and he will reign over the house of Jacob forever, and of his kingdom there will be no end" (Luke 1:30–33).

In this one short announcement, the angel Gabriel has just taken the entire package of Old Testament kingdom-prophecy and dropped it on young astonished Mary. "Your son is the One," he is saying. "Your son is the Seed of the woman, your son is the One who reigns from the River to the ends of the earth; your son is the One whose kingdom will fill the earth as God promised through Daniel. Your son is the Child of Isaiah 9!"

All this and much more lies back of Jesus' proclamation as we return finally to Mark 1 and listen again to him say, "The time has been fulfilled." He is saying quite simply that the decisive threshold of fulfillment of everything spoken by the law and the prophets has already been crossed. That is the force of the verb he uses here. The sense is not, "The time is *about* to be fulfilled." It is not even, "The time is presently *being* fulfilled." It is rather, "The time *has been* fulfilled."

The decisive threshold of the fulfillment of all the Old Covenant promises has already been crossed. It is now already God's appointed time to visit mankind, to set up a kingdom of righteousness and peace that will never end and indeed will fill the earth, replacing universal cursing with universal blessing. It is now already God's appointed time to enthrone the anointed son of David, who is both the Son of God and the Son of Man as the law and the prophets told us, who is Jesus himself, the God-Man. It is now already God's appointed time to restore human dominion over the earth and human communion with God. It is *already here*, that is what Jesus is saying. We must try to imagine how this would have thrilled the heart of a Jew who really knew the Old Covenant Scriptures – if he or she could even have taken it all in!

Then there is this curious language, "The kingdom of God has come near." This is probably a better rendering than "is at hand," because "is at hand" could still leave a sense that the thing is *about* to happen, *about* to arrive. No, the kingdom of God has drawn near; the verb Jesus chooses means that the thing of which he speaks is already definitively here. The preceding phrase established this: the time *has been* fulfilled; and in that fulfillment the kingdom of God *has come* near. But this is still an interesting verb to choose, "has come near," because it leaves open the possibility that the kingdom of God may have come near in less-than-full form. Let me try to explain.

To come near is not necessarily, as of yet, to fill and dominate the scene. A thing may already have come near without yet having taken the whole of the stage. The possibility is left open in the word Jesus chooses that the kingdom, though *definitively* present, may not be manifested *in its fullness all at once*. And this is fairly obvious, when you think about it: clearly not every enemy of the God-Man, the Son of David, is already visibly under his feet when Jesus makes this announcement. As of the moment Jesus speaks, the kingdom has already come near, but it is not yet in its full expression as it will be in time to come.

Let us see where we are now. We know from Old Covenant prophecy something of the scope of what the kingdom entails. We know from Jesus that the time of the fulfillment of Old Covenant kingdom-prophecy has already decisively arrived. In the remainder of this series of studies, I want to explore with you what it means that the kingdom has "drawn near," *in what form* the kingdom manifests itself – in Jesus' time, in our own time, and in the future. But for the present, let us turn to our second question.

WHAT DOES JESUS SAY IS THE PROPER RESPONSE TO THE GOSPEL?

Jesus says the content of the gospel is the kingdom of God. We need to let this sink in. If, when we talk to people about the gospel, we don't talk to them about the kingdom of God, we are not talking about the Christian gospel, because Jesus said the gospel, the glad tidings, is the kingdom of God. We must bring something of this central idea and reality into our communication of the gospel to other people.

What does Jesus say is the proper response to his glad tidings? Even without having fully explored the form the kingdom took in Jesus' time and in the time of the apostles; even without having studied the form in which it presents itself in our time; and even without having contemplated the form in which it will be manifested in the future, we have cleared enough ground to understand and take to heart what Jesus intends when he says, "Repent and believe in the glad tidings [of the kingdom of God]."

One thing is immediately obvious. In the mind of our Lord, the kingdom of God and the announcement of that kingdom are not mere information. This is no infomercial: "We interrupt the normal broadcasting of your life to announce that the kingdom of God has come near. Thank you. We now resume our normal broadcasting." That is *not* what is going on. This is an announcement of divine activity, of kingdom-building activity that embraces the whole of creation within its scope (think back to the prophecies of the Old Testament); and in the face of this announcement, no passive neutrality is possible. Jesus says, "Turn and believe, for God is acting! God is building a kingdom. In fact, he has already acted and the kingdom is here. So you must act. You must turn and believe." Passive neutrality is impossible in response to this message.

Think with me further about how Jesus' summons flows out of his announcement of the kingdom. The kingdom of God is divine activity. It is God's active response of saving grace toward those who have rejected his rule (think back to Genesis 3:15). It is the aggressive outworking of his great master plan to restore his creation – to restore individual lives, families, communities, even structures of civilization. It is the active outworking of his purpose to overturn the curse and ruin brought upon humankind by Adam's rebellion. This is a message saturated with astonishing grace. And to ignore this message – to have no response, or an apathetic response – is active rebellion against the purpose and working of the King. If you and I don't turn and believe this good news, we are simply at war with God. Jesus in these glad tidings issues a clarion summons, and he will not be ignored. What does he mean by the word "repent"? He means that we are to *turn*. Turn from what?

We are to turn away from all other *would-be saviors*. How our world needs to hear this today! Turn away, humankind, from all other would-be saviors! You lie under the curse of God and the ruin and the misery brought by Adam's sin, and it matters not how much education or political savvy or military prowess or self-improvement counseling you have, there is no hope for you outside Jesus Christ and the kingdom of God that he brings. No one and nothing else can reconcile you to God; no one and nothing else can restore your lives, your homes, or your communities, or put the world as a whole back together. There is no other name given under heaven by which we can be saved except Jesus alone. He comes and says, "Repent! Turn! I am the only one who can deliver you from God's curse and from all your ruin on account of that curse."

There is more to this turning. We are to turn away from all other *sovereigns*. Jesus alone has the right to claim our ultimate allegiance, and he is to receive it. It is astonishing what a struggle is required at times to convince, not those outside the church, but those *within* the church that they actually owe Jesus something. It comes as a fairly radical insight to many professing Christians that Jesus is their King; that when he speaks, it is their duty to know what he says, and to respond with an immediate and cheerful "Yes, Lord." We will have cause to revisit this again in a future study.

We are told to turn from all other would-be saviors and sovereigns and to *believe* Jesus' glad tidings. The word carries the idea of radical self-entrustment; we are to venture our souls on this message and on the Messenger who embodies it, upon this one and only King of kings. Only this King will save us. Only this King shall rule us.

Actually, Jesus does not say, "believe," as if his good news were mere information; he says, "believe *in*." If one may so express it, all our eggs are to be in the one basket of this kingdom administered by Jesus, God's Son and God's Anointed. Each of us must turn and submit individually to his gracious, saving rule; to do otherwise is, as noted before, to be at war with the King of kings. He is not a salesman on our doorstep, hoping to pitch his wares. He is a King summoning the world to come to him for life and hope and restoration. That is how he speaks.

CONCLUSION

We close by reflecting again on the shaping power of this great biblical idea of the kingdom of God; which is no mere idea but an actual, present, active reality in our world right now, whether we happen to believe in it or not. And it has massive implications for the way we think and live in our tiny everyday existences. The biblical idea of the kingdom should shape and expand our thinking in at least two ways:

(1) *It should shape our thinking about history.* On August 8, 2008, millions watched the opening program of the Beijing Olympics. It was, aesthetically and artistically speaking, a truly overwhelming event. But it was also painful as a Christian to listen to commentators speak of these Olympics as a significant step toward world peace and order. Let it be said, gathering the athletes of 204 nations together to play sports is not going to heal and reunite our fractured world. That blessed hope will be realized only in and through the kingdom of God.

This being the case, the really exciting news on the world scene is that the kingdom of God has arrived! And as noted above, we are living in the historical unfolding of that kingdom whether we believe it or not, whether we like it or not. We are living in the historical unfolding of that kingdom *today*. This means that our lives are not just *happening*. Life is not just happening. Our lives are unfolding as one small part of God's kingdom plan. And this, in turn, means that our lives are fraught with moral significance, because at every moment we are either actively serving the King or we are actively warring against him.

We tend to "narrate" the world, to tell the story of the world in our minds, in terms of how the world revolves around *us*, what we feel, what we want, what we enjoy. Jesus' announcement of the kingdom of God means that we need to "re-narrate" the world in terms of how it revolves around the reign of God in the earth, around his sovereignty, around his salvation, around what he is doing in the earth.

(2) *It should shape our thinking about God.* Perhaps some of what has been said above sounds harsh or distasteful. We are not very much accustomed to having the place of sovereignty in our lives claimed by another. Does it thrill your heart to hear the words (and to say them yourself), "Our God reigns"? Do you think of your God that way, as the reigning God? Does God reign in your life? And if he does, does that comfort you? Does it reassure you? Does it delight you?

For many saints the statement "Jesus is Lord" sits uncomfortably with the statement "Jesus is Savior." The statement "Jesus is Lord" sounds like legalism; "Jesus is Savior" sounds like grace. But there is something distorted in such thinking. Why do we fear the announcement, "Your God reigns [and reigns over you]"? Why do we fear the idea of the Lordship of Jesus? Why should it sit ill with us that when Jesus speaks (and he does!) we are to submit to him, wholly, without reserve, without question?

We need to think about these questions, because if Jesus is not the Lord of all, then he cannot be our Savior. Have you ever thought about that? If your God does not reign, you cannot be certain he will conquer your enemies; you may be as sure of his delivering you from the dominion of Satan as you are of the outcome of a coin toss. It is precisely the announcement that our God reigns "from the River to the ends of the earth" that enables us to say confidently, "I shall be saved from all my enemies."

There is more, which we will explore further in the next study: The King who speaks this day in Galilee is a sweet, gracious, kind, and good king. He is the *best* king, all of whose omnipotence is bent upon blessing you now and forever. That is the kind of king he is. Noble? Yes. Omnipotent? Yes. Fierce? Yes. Ferocious against his enemies? Yes. He is the Lion of the tribe of Judah. When he roars, the earth shakes. Never think of him as anything less. He is not safe, but he is exceedingly good. Infinitely good.

In fact, when the biblical prophet wants to comfort God's discouraged people, he cannot think of any better message than these precious words with which I want to close: "How beautiful upon the mountains are the feet of him who brings good news, who publishes peace [*shalom*], who brings good news of happiness, who publishes [not judgment but] salvation, who says to Zion, 'Your God reigns' " (Isaiah 52:7). May the Lord fit our hearts to such a message as this.

CHAPTER TWO

THE KINGDOM
AND THE SINNER

Scripture Readings:

Numbers 2:1–34

Luke 1:67–79

INTRODUCTION

I want to begin this study with a short summary of the last one. We can sum up what we learned from the Lord Jesus in Mark 1:14–15 in four propositions:

1) According to Jesus, the kingdom of God *is* the "gospel." (We may not think of the kingdom when we think about the Christian gospel, but Jesus said the kingdom of God – the arrival and outworking of this glorious reality – is the gospel, the glad tidings.)

2) The "kingdom of God," which Jesus himself does not define in Mark 1:14–15, is defined by Old Covenant promises and prophesies, flowing out of the covenant God made with Abraham, which point forward to the rule of a Child of the line of David, who will be God himself (the "Mighty God," as Isaiah said) and through whom righteousness and peace will flow to all nations.

3) This prophesied Child is the Lord Jesus Christ; recall that the angel Gabriel said as much to Mary. In him the kingdom of God has *already* arrived in human history.

4) The proper response to the glad tidings of the kingdom is to turn from all other would-be saviors and sovereigns, and radically to entrust oneself to Jesus as the only Savior-King.

Note that Jesus' statement in Mark 1, "the kingdom of God has drawn near," especially when interpreted in the light of the rest of the New Testament, lays to rest at least one idea that continues to find acceptance even in Reformed churches, namely, that the kingdom of God is something to be expected almost entirely in the *future* – even more particularly, that the great hope of the coming of God's kingdom to earth lies in a future "millennium" or thousand-year reign of Christ. Of course, Dispensationalists believe that a millennial kingdom will be established on earth after God "raptures" the church; but not a few people in Reformed churches also believe that God's kingdom, at least in any truly meaningful form, is yet to arrive in the future. Jesus flatly dispels such a notion. The kingdom of God is *now*. It is actually, emphatically, and meaningfully *here*.

However, Jesus' statement in Mark 1 does leave open a significant question, which we noted in our last study: What *form* does God's kingdom take in history (in Jesus' time and beyond)? Until we answer this question, it will not be clear just how we are to respond concretely to the kingdom and to Jesus' kingly rule. Jesus said, "Repent, turn, and believe in the kingdom," but Jesus doesn't have an army or an air force in which you and I can enlist; we don't find recruiters for the kingdom of God banging on our front doors, urging us to sign up. What does it look like *concretely* to turn at the sound of the glad tidings of the kingdom and to do something with that good news? To answer such questions, we must first know what form the kingdom takes in history.

In this study I want to focus on the form the kingdom took in the period covered by the four Gospel accounts, because the kingdom-form in the Gospels is foundational to everything else in kingdom history, right up to the moment you read this, and beyond.

The Gospels, as you know, give us the history of the King. They tell us the story of how Jesus the King inaugurated, ushered in, and set up the kingdom of God. But this story, you have no doubt noticed, is full of surprises. Think about it. What ordinarily happens when kings go forth to assert their rule? In *The Lord of the Rings*, what happens when Aragorn or Théoden or the Lord of the Nazgûl goes forth to press his kingly claims? Armies go marching: recall the wildly affecting scene in *The Two Towers* in which we hear the quickstep of the Uruk-hai, marching forth under Saruman the White. Not only armies but also cavalry, like the Rohirrim, thunder across the plains to battle. When kings go forth, there are sweeping military maneuvers; there are flags and standards; there are swords loud clashing and the roll of stirring drums. That's how kingdoms come. But when you read the Gospels, there is really none of this as the King brings in his kingdom. There is rather – and it is somewhat unsettling – a long, slow march . . . to a Roman cross. Not without reason Martin Kähler once brilliantly described the Gospels as "passion narratives with extended introductions," for in reality every one of the four Gospels is primarily about the passion – the death and resurrection – of Jesus Christ; all that precedes in the Gospel accounts is in one sense merely introductory. It is to the *passion* that the history of the King leads us.

In light of this, let us come finally to our text, Zacharias' prophecy in Luke 1:68–79, and observe together two blessings that the kingdom of God brings.

THE KINGDOM BRINGS
FORGIVENESS OF SINS

Luke, as he goes about writing his Gospel, his "passion narrative with an extended introduction," places the *Benedictus* of Zacharias very early, in chapter one. The reason for this is that the *Benedictus*, a poetic prophecy, really sets the program for the remainder of Luke's Gospel. If you want to know what the Gospel of Luke is about, you would do well to begin here in this first chapter and with this prophecy in particular.

Notice that the first half of Zacharias' beautiful, Spirit-inspired poem situates the history of Jesus squarely in the context of Old Testament kingdom prophecies, for he says in verse 69 that God has "raised up a horn of salvation for us." Perhaps this doesn't ring many bells for us twenty-first century Americans, but it is an image of a mighty ram's horn being lifted up in victory. When rams dispute over territory, they charge each other and bash heads, and the ram with the bigger horn prevails. This image actually comes up quite often in the Old Testament (e.g., Psalm 18:2; 75:4–5; 89:17, 24; 92:10; 112:9; 132:17; 148:14; Jeremiah 48:25; Ezekiel 29:21; Daniel 7:8, 11, 20–21; 8:5, 8–9, 21–22; Micah 4:13), and here God has "raised up a horn of salvation" in the house of his servant David, because David is the king, and his house is the king's house.

God has raised up a horn of salvation, Zacharias says, "just as he spoke" (verse 70); indeed, God has been announcing this event "by the mouth of his holy prophets from of old," since the world began. In a stroke, the Holy Spirit here tells us, "If you want to understand the Old Testament, you must understand that it all points forward to God's raising up a horn of salvation by raising up a king from the kingly line of David. That is what the whole Old Testament was moving toward."

The long-promised kingdom, the Holy Spirit tells us through Zacharias, has arrived; God has already raised up the horn of salvation. In fact, we already know this from an earlier part of chapter one in which God through the angel Gabriel tells Mary that her son Jesus "will be great and will be called the Son of the Most High. And the Lord God will give to him the throne of his father David, and he will reign over the house of Jacob forever, and of his kingdom there will be no end" (verses 32–33).

The kingdom that comes in Jesus is the kingdom of Old Testament prophecy. It has now arrived, and the Holy Spirit through Zacharias says this entails nothing less – the kingdom brings nothing less – than *full deliverance from every one of the enemies of God's people* (verse 71). This is the essence of what the kingdom brings: "that we should be saved from our enemies and from the hand of all who hate us."

So far, we are on ground that is fairly familiar from our first study; but then look at the second half of Zacharias' poem, beginning in verse 76. The second half of the poem tells us *how concretely* the kingdom of God saves us from all of our enemies. It identifies the salvation that will be brought by the king (the horn of salvation in the house of David) as "the forgiveness [or the remission] of their sins" (verse 77). "You, John," says Zacharias, "are going to give the knowledge of salvation to God's people, and this is what the salvation given by God through their king will look like: it will consist in the taking away of their sins."

Think about this. What does the forgiveness of our sins have to do with deliverance from all of our enemies? What can forgiveness possibly have to do with God's delivering his people from all of their enemies?

To answer that question, we must ponder for a moment who or what are our enemies. Who are your enemies? The Jews of Jesus' day would have immediately mentioned political oppressors, the Gentile domination under which they were languishing. We modern Americans, if we were to start cataloging our enemies, might mention things such as stress, or big oil companies, or Al Qaeda, or whoever stands between us and our 70-inch plasma TV. Who or what are your enemies?

I will tell you one you probably wouldn't immediately think of. What about *God?* You may say, "Oh, God would never be my enemy." *Au contraire*. Paul says, "While we were enemies we were reconciled to God by the death of his Son" (Romans 5:10).

May I say to you, very plainly, that if God is your enemy, it doesn't matter who your friends are. It doesn't matter who your allies are. You may marshal every army in heaven and earth to your side, but we are speaking of the God who utters his voice and the earth melts before him; the God who gazes upon the swirling galaxies of an uncharted universe as mere playthings; the God who settled the mountains of old and walks in the depths of the sea; the God who can cast not merely the body but body and soul into hell. There are no allies against this Enemy, for none can stand before him when once he is angry (Psalm 76:7). He is of purer eyes than to look upon sin, and if he looks upon you and beholds anything less than the perfection for which he created you and which he righteously demands of you according to his most holy law, then you are his enemy. And that, though few think of it as such, is an exceedingly serious problem. There is, indeed, none more serious. There is no more fearful enemy of sinful man than he.

Another enemy we might not often think about: What about *Satan*? I am puzzled when Reformed Christians seem uncomfortable talking about Satan. I wonder if some of us even believe he really exists, but let us here expand our minds to embrace the biblical witness. The Bible tells us that the entire sphere of human accursedness, the entire sphere of human life that lies under God's judicial curse, the entire sphere in which humankind live in ruinous estrangement from their Creator – that entire sphere of human life is one in which the destroying agenda of Satan dominates and reigns.

Now we don't *see* Satan. We don't see Satan's devils. We don't see the human enslavement that results from estrangement from God – we don't see people walking around in shackles, driven by the whips of dark taskmasters. These are not visible things, but nevertheless Scripture tells us quite plainly that the whole sphere of life in which men and women and boys and girls are estranged from their God, living under his curse, living as his enemies, is a domain over which Satan rules, in which he presses his destroying agenda. In that realm, he incites men to draw down upon them God's curse. He incites them to sin more and more; and he doesn't have to work very hard at this, does he? He merely pulls the strings of lust, the strings of that earnest desire in the fallen human heart to live as far away from God as possible, and men and women and boys and girls willingly dance their way, like stupid puppets, toward eternal destruction. This is a *real* domain. You may not like how I've described it. You may think of more precise metaphors to express the reality, but it is a reality the Scriptures undeniably disclose. There *is* a kingdom of darkness over which Satan holds sway.

You and I usually define or think of our enemies (if we ever think of our enemies) in terms of the various and sundry miseries of this life, which are very real. But in our text, the Holy Spirit through Zacharias takes us far upstream and shows us that all miseries – and death itself, that supreme enemy and misery of humankind – flow from a preceding and more fundamental *curse of God* upon humankind, which can be removed only by the forgiveness of sins. And so, with all of this in mind, the history of our King in Luke's Gospel and in the other Gospels has two focal points:

One focal point is to remove the curse of God. The King throughout the history set forth in the Gospels is on his way to give his life as a redemption price to God. That is the significance of the cross: my curse and your curse on Jesus, as he dies accursed in our place on the cross, paying the price to release us from death. That is one focal point.

The other focal point is to cast down the prince of darkness. Jesus says, "If it is by the finger of God that I cast out demons, then the kingdom of God has come upon you" (Luke 11:20). And at the very threshold of the cross, the very threshold of the passion narrative, he says, "Now is the judgment of this world [the cosmos over which Satan has claimed jurisdiction]. Now will the ruler of this world be cast out" (John 12:31).

What the Gospels are telling us is that, because the curse of God has been removed in the cross, there is no more death for God's people; and because there is no more death for God's people, the one who has the power of death has been disarmed. Satan's power over those for whom Jesus died has been definitively broken: he can no longer steal; he can no longer kill; he cannot destroy anymore. His weapons have been snatched out of his hands and nailed to the cross (Colossians 2:14–15), and we have been released. And so we see that the death of the King around which the Gospels center (that strangest of all kingdom events!), and the full forgiveness of sins secured in his death, *really do* deliver us from all of our enemies; for in the death and resurrection of our King we have the guarantee that, though we don't see it yet in full, every vestige of God's curse upon us, every misery we endure on account of that curse, will assuredly be removed.

This is why, in the Old Testament, the central kingdom reality is not perimeter fortresses all around the outside of Palestine ("Look, we've got the highest walls in the Middle East!"). It is not some glorious kingly palace, or mighty garrisons of armies. The central kingdom reality in the Old Testament is the *place of atonement* (recall from our reading in Numbers 2 how the tribes of Israel were arranged around the tabernacle). In this kingdom, God through the blood sacrifices (which point to the death of the coming King) reconciles man to himself; this kingdom people, because of the shedding of blood, is no longer under his curse. *That* is a central reality of the kingdom.

Paul likewise tells us in Colossians 1:13–14, "[God] has delivered us from the domain of darkness and transferred us to the kingdom of his beloved Son." What is the fundamental blessing of this kingdom? "In whom we have redemption [the redemption price is paid in Jesus' blood], the forgiveness of sins." That which God identifies as the central reality of his kingdom is the forgiveness of sins, the removal of his curse.

What is emerging here is that the kingdom is first – and we need to pay attention to this carefully – something *invisible*. We may perhaps want to run immediately to some visible manifestation, some visible form, of the kingdom; but that would profoundly miss the fundamental biblical truth about the kingdom of God. It is first something we *don't* see; when we think about the kingdom of God, the first thing we must think of is God's definitive reassertion of his dominion in the invisible sphere of spiritual powers.

God has entered into the heavens. He has taken up the sword and bared his mighty arm, and he has shattered the powers of darkness that hold his creation captive – and this invisible warfare is where the sound of marching and the thunder of rolling drums is heard in the Gospels. The King has entered the heavenly places and has thrown down the prince of darkness and released humankind. Deliverance from our visible enemies, though the Jews of Jesus' day could not see this (and frankly, often neither do we), is a byproduct of deliverance from our invisible enemies.

We might think of this in connection with the current conflicts in the Middle East (where many Americans might identify certain visible enemies). What would happen if God were to raise up a few young men, full of the Holy Spirit, and send them to the Middle East, and they were to invade Muslim countries with the gospel of Jesus Christ? What if they began preaching in that place the glad tidings that Jesus has thrown down the powers of darkness, doing what Mohammad could never do, ransoming and redeeming the people of God? What if they were to proclaim that Jesus is the true prophet of God in whom the glad tidings of release from our spiritual bondage are proclaimed to every nation under the sun; that Mohammad is a fraud, and Jesus is the only Savior-King? Suppose God blessed their ministry and their preaching were so accompanied by the power of the Spirit that men and women and boys and girls in that troubled region began to be converted and to realize, "Jesus is our great Savior! He is the great King and Prophet and Priest of God. He has set us free." Do you know what would begin to happen over time in that place? These awakened souls would begin to gather under the preaching of the Word and to realize, "We are brethren. We have been reconciled to God as our Father, and now we are brethren." They would lay down their arms and shut down their tanks and bury their rockets, and begin building churches and building a civilization in which there is real peace. This would be the glorious result. The forces of the United Nations are never going to counterfeit the work that God alone can do! Deliverance from our visible enemies is a byproduct of the invisible shattering of the powers of darkness through the death and resurrection of Jesus Christ. It is neither a small nor a peripheral thing that the first blessing the kingdom brings is the forgiveness of sins. But let us come to the second blessing.

THE KINGDOM BRINGS SERVICE TO GOD

In addition to forgiveness of sins, the kingdom brings service to God. We have been saved, says Zacharias (verse 74), "from the hand of our enemies, [in order that] we might serve [God] without fear, in holiness and righteousness before him all our days."

I think we often do not realize how radical it is that we have been saved from *all* of our enemies. We have not just been saved from death — that awful, hellish *end of life* in Satan's kingdom. We have been saved from that, all praise to our God! But we have also been saved from the whole *way of life* in that kingdom. We have been saved from life without God as our Father and our King. We have been saved from an orphaned life, which is what life outside God's kingdom really is. We have been saved from that independent way of life which is a highway to hell regardless of how nice and tidy it may appear on the outside. God will not rest until every ruinous trace of life in Satan's kingdom is purged out of our lives and our whole lives are restored to the glory he intended for humankind at creation. God will not merely give pardoning grace. He does give pardoning grace, surely, but he will never give anyone *only* pardoning grace. He will also, assuredly, give *renovating* grace to put our lives back together through the power of his Spirit.

Can you imagine what a living death it would be to be delivered from death itself, delivered from everlasting death in hell, but not to be brought again under God's loving rule, rather simply left to self-rule? Would not such "deliverance" throw us into the very existence apart from God which is basic to hell? Imagine if God were to say to you, "Here is your get-out-of-hell-free card. I've signed your hell-insurance contract. And now henceforth no will shall rule you except your own. Your only master shall be your desire. No law of love shall bind you, only the law of your own self-pleasing." Could you speak of God as your Savior if he were to do this? Certainly not! He would not have saved you, for in that moment he would have turned you over to another kind of hell.

But this idea is nonsense. We have been saved into a kingdom where we have a *King*, who does not simply deliver us and defend us but also rules us — and this is good news! Indeed, it is wonderful news! And we should study his good laws in order that we might walk in his good ways, learning what it means concretely to love him with all that we are and all that we have, and learning how to love our neighbors as ourselves.

Zacharias articulates this in terms of "serving before" our King. This is not just a generic term, it is again an image drawn from the

Old Testament. You will recall that around the Old Testament tabernacle constructed under Moses, there was an outer court. Levites could go into this outer court. Then there was the tabernacle itself, a smaller curtained structure, where only priests could enter. Within the tabernacle was a partitioned area called the Most Holy Place, and here only the high priest could enter once a year, with blood, on the Day of Atonement. Do you realize what Zacharias is picturing for us when he says, "that we . . . might serve him without fear, in holiness and righteousness before him"? The language of service is *priestly* language (e.g., Numbers 16:9; Psalm 134:1–2). The Holy Spirit is in effect saying, "I have taken down the outer curtain of the tabernacle. I have taken down the curtains of the tabernacle itself. I have torn apart and thrown away the veil that was before the Most Holy Place – and now the entire kingdom of God's people are priests with access to the Most Holy Place." And in this kingdom – which is all Most Holy – we serve our God without fear, in righteousness and holiness, in community as priests all our days.

Having explored the two kingdom-blessings prophesied (or, perhaps better, announced) by Zacharias, let us move quickly now to an important question:

HOW ARE THESE KINGDOM BLESSINGS CONNECTED?

Perhaps you have already been wondering, "How are these two kingdom blessings connected? How do they relate to each other?" I myself have wrestled with this. How are *forgiveness* and *service* to be connected without canceling each other out? How can we hold together the ideas that Jesus is Savior (who gives forgiveness of sins) and that Jesus is Lord (who rules over us, and whom we are to serve)? Some of you may think, as I have, "As soon as I stop thinking about Jesus as my Savior and start thinking of him as my Lord, I feel as if I am immediately in bondage all over again, trying to maintain God's mercy and grace by my obedience, and under God's anger when I don't obey (which is often). I'm right back into the whole business of works-righteousness."

Do you know what such thinking says about us? It says that we don't, first of all, really believe Jesus has saved us from the penalty of sin. It means we don't really believe Jesus has truly saved us – not merely *moved us towards* being saved, but *saved* us from the penalty of sin – because we are still trying to add to his saving work by our works.

But such thinking says something else about us as well. It says that we don't yet understand, as we should, how glorious it is that Jesus has saved us not only from the *penalty* of sin but also from the *power* and the *practice* of sin. In fact, can we see that to say "Jesus is Lord" *is* to speak of him as Savior? Let us revisit the gospel again:

The good news is that our King destroyed death because he absorbed in full the curse of God upon our sins. God "laid on him the iniquity of us all" (Isaiah 53:6), and we need to put our feet down on this and say, "This is more true than my feelings. The veil that separates me from God has been torn. The Almighty who cannot lie has said so. What pours out of the Most Holy Place now is not wrath that drives me from God. It is infinite, unbounded, inexhaustible, everlasting, unchangeable, faithful love. That is what gushes out of the Holiest Place, from behind the torn veil."

But, as I have already said, the love that pours out of the Most Holy Place is not content that we should go forth and live as vagabonds and wanderers in the earth. The love of God wills to undo *all* of the ruin wrought in us by sin and Satan. It wills to usher us into the fullness of *communion* with our God – walking and fellowshipping with him. It wills moreover to usher us into the fullness of *dominion* over the earth; into the task, as co-laborers with God, of spreading the rule of his love and grace and righteousness and truth to the four corners of the earth. Our loving King wills thus to govern our lives; and these expressions of his gracious rule are part of what it means that he is our Savior.

The point of connection between the blessings of forgiveness and service is this: When we understand the gospel – the fullness of salvation secured in the death of our King – that understanding will melt the natural icy enmity in our hearts against our God. The sunlight of the love of God will invade our inmost hearts. It will emancipate us from unholy fear and dread of God. It will woo us with grace until our very motivational structures are turned upside down. It really will. The love of God in Christ will make us *want nothing more* than to live forever worshiping his glory, pouring out our love at his feet, and watering the world with his love and grace and righteousness and truth.

It is true that God wills (and he will not be turned away!) that we submit to his law. That is a lost doctrine in the church today. God wills for our good that we submit to every one of his righteous laws, but he wills that we always *receive his law in the nail-pierced hands of our Redeemer.* We don't receive the law from thundering Sinai anymore. We receive the law as it comes to us in the hands of our wounded Savior – it is *he* who delivers to us the law; and that makes all the difference.

In his commentary on Psalm 130, John Owens writes these beautiful words:

> [Closing with forgiveness, believing the gospel, believing in the forgiveness of sins] will give you such motives, such encouragements, as will greatly influence your hearts and souls. It will give you freedom, liberty, delight, and cheerfulness, in all duties of gospel obedience. You will find a constraining power in the love of Christ therein, – a freedom from bondage, when the Son truly hath made you free. Faith and love will work genuinely and naturally in your spirits; and that which was your greatest burden will become your chiefest joy, 2 Cor. vii. 1. Thoughts of the love of God, of the blood of Christ, or of the covenant of grace [*we might add, the kingdom of God*], and [a] sense of pardon in them, will enlarge your hearts and sweeten all your duties. [*Our duties may at times be hard, but when we are in love with God, we want to do them.*] You will find a new life, a new pleasure, a new satisfaction, in all that you do.[5]

CONCLUSION

Our next study will explore how we as God's people begin working out the implications of these gladsome, life-giving tidings as we fulfill our calling to rebuild the city of God in the midst of our dying world. May the Lord bless these things to our hearts.

CHAPTER THREE

THE KINGDOM
AND THE CHURCH

Scripture Readings:

Isaiah 22:15–24

Matthew 16:13–28

Matthew 28:16–20

INTRODUCTION

Let us take a moment to see where we are as we begin. In our first study we learned from Jesus (Mark 1:14–15) that if we wish to try to capture the "gospel" in a nutshell, it is this: that the time has been fulfilled, and the kingdom of God has come to earth. The kingdom long awaited by the Old Testament prophets is here; it has now burst into the world in the Person of Jesus Christ.

In our second study we saw that, in the four Gospels, the arrival of God's kingdom is manifested in the death of the King for his people. A strange way, surely, for a kingdom to arrive – puzzlingly unlike any other kingdom ever heard of – but, in the wisdom of God, this is just what sets his kingdom apart from all other kingdoms. The death of the righteous King in the place of his unrighteous subjects redeems them from slavery in the kingdom of darkness by releasing them from accursedness under the righteous judgment of God. As Zacharias prophesied (Luke 1:68–79), the salvation of God that arrives with his kingdom can be summed up in "the forgiveness of [our] sins"; and this forgiveness of sins and deliverance from God's curse upon us has also freed us from the destroyer of our souls, Satan, who accuses, steals, and kills. He cannot harm us anymore, because our curse has been taken out of the way by King Jesus.

God has saved us from his own wrath through the death of the King. He has saved us from Satan and the dominion of the destroyer. He has delivered us, in truth, from *all* of our enemies; for now it is really just a matter of time (since Jesus' resurrection) until every misery we endure as a result of God's curse upon sin is fully taken out of the way, fully removed not only from us but also from our whole environment in heaven and on earth. And God's purpose in liberating us from all our enemies, as Zacharias announced, is that, having finally been brought back to our God, we might serve in his presence in holiness and righteousness without fear. These are blessed things!

Also in the four Gospels, as we turn now to our third study, the King begins to tell us what *form* the kingdom of God will take after his death and resurrection. We cannot talk about the kingdom of God in any meaningful way unless we understand the death and resurrection of Jesus; those events are the great cornerstone of the kingdom. But

Jesus also begins to tell us what form God's kingdom will take upon the earth after he has died and been raised. Listen to Geerhardus Vos: "Towards the close of His ministry our Lord opened up the prospect of a new form of development upon which in result of His death and glorification the spiritual kingdom would enter. This is the church (cf. Matt. 16:18, 19)."[6] Vos references our text in Matthew 16, so let us examine it more closely.

The upshot of Matthew 16:18–19 is that God's heavenly kingdom, as Vos said, is going to take earthly visible form in the *church*. Even on the surface of the verses, you can see this immediately. How is Jesus going to build his church? He says, "I will build my church" (verse 18); *how* is he going to do it? By giving Peter the keys of the kingdom. As Peter wields the keys of the heavenly kingdom, Jesus will cause that invisible kingdom of God – that rule of God we don't see with our physical eyes – to take visible shape in the building of what he calls here "my church." The kingdom of heaven is going to be manifested, visibly, in this lively edifice called the church.

We need to pause and reflect on this, because we don't tend to think of the church as a kingdom. (In fact, we Americans don't understand the idea of kingdom very well at all. We have for a long time taken pride in not having a king!) A great many of us probably think of the church more as a spiritual spa: we go to church because we realize from time to time that our spiritual lives and looks need some kind of improvement – a bit of exercise, perhaps, to get back in shape. At best, we often think of the church as a kind of medical clinic: things are falling apart, so we'd better get to church; we'd better go talk to the pastor or elders and get some help solving our current crises and problems.

But the church is not a spiritual spa, and it is not a medical clinic. It is a sphere of *dominion*, and we are never outside this sphere of dominion. We have certain blessings and certain obligations because we are in the sphere of God's dominion, and these blessings and obligations are ours *all the time*, not just when we are having a problem and feel the need to run to the church.

I want to unpack Matthew 16:18–19, and also a few verses in Matthew 28, by making just two points: (1) The King's rule is (or becomes) visible in the ordinances of his church. (2) The King's rule is visible in the obedience of his church.

THE KING'S RULE IS VISIBLE IN THE ORDINANCES OF HIS CHURCH

First, let us consider the ordinances of the church. Here I must speak somewhat bluntly: we Protestants have long been defensive about Matthew 16:18–19 because the Church of Rome wants to say, based on this text, that Peter is the first pope. We have gotten so defensive about the text that I think we've missed how shocking it really is!

Jesus says to this man, Simon Peter, "I am going to give into your hands the keys of the kingdom of God. What this means is that you are going to loose men by admitting them through the gates of the kingdom; you will free men, as my representative, by admitting them into my kingdom. And you are going to bind other men by shutting them out, by refusing them admittance to my kingdom." Now that in itself is pretty heady stuff, but then notice what Jesus says at the end of verse 19. He tells Peter, "Whatever you bind on earth will have been bound in heaven, and whatever you loose on earth will have been loosed in heaven. As if what I just said were not amazing enough, Peter, your actions on the earth will correspond to my actions in heaven itself." *What is going on here?* How can Jesus give this kind of power to a mere man?

Look at the context. What has just occurred? Peter (verse 16) has just grasped the gospel. The "good news" has just been revealed to him by none other than the Father in heaven. He has just confessed, "Jesus, you are the Christ, the Messiah, the Anointed One of God. You are the Son of the living God. You are the one all the prophets have been talking about, the one who brings the kingdom and salvation of God! You are not like John the Baptizer, or Elijah, or Jeremiah – men who spoke of the Coming One. Jesus, you *are* the Coming One!" And in this moment of divine illumination Jesus, the King of the kingdom, appoints Peter and says to him, "You, Peter, are going to stand at the gates of my kingdom with this good news; and you are officially going to open the gates to all who receive the glad tidings that *I am he*, that I am the Messiah. To all who receive this gospel, Peter, and to their households, you are to open the gates of the kingdom, loosing them and letting them come in. Moreover, Peter, as you stand at the gates with the gospel, you are going to shut the kingdom of heaven against all who reject this gospel."

Think with me about this for a moment. What is Jesus saying? He is saying that Peter, *by faithfully preaching the pure gospel message of salvation through Jesus alone* – the message that there is no other name given under heaven by which we are saved; that Jesus alone saves; that we are saved when we throw ourselves upon him alone, without any works of our own; that salvation is free, because Jesus has done it all – by faithfully preaching this message at the gates of the kingdom, Peter will *in the message itself* officially open the gates to some and shut the gates to others.

And isn't that, in fact, just what Peter does on the Day of Pentecost? When suddenly the Spirit falls from heaven, and God is doing unbelievable things, and men and women are speaking in tongues, Peter begins to preach the gospel and his hearers are cut to the heart and cry out, saying, "What must we do?" Their question is, "How shall we get into the kingdom? How do we partake of the salvation of God, Peter?" And Peter, the great gatekeeper of the kingdom of God, says, "This is what you must do. You must turn. You must come to Jesus. You must be baptized in the name of Jesus Christ for the forgiveness of your sins. In Jesus alone there is forgiveness. You are to come, and in faith you and your households are to be baptized. The water of baptism pouring over you is to signify what Jesus does for his people: he washes them from their sins. You are to come by faith. This is how you will save yourself from this wicked generation" (see Acts 2:37–40). He is saying to the Jews as the gatekeeper of the kingdom, "Jesus is the only way in." In so doing, he has opened the door to those who will come by Jesus. He has slammed the gate shut against those who will not come by Jesus. And his judgment in so doing agrees with God's heavenly judgment, because God has already spoken from heaven: in the early chapters of Matthew's Gospel, God said by the angel Gabriel to Joseph, "You shall name this Child Jesus, for he [and by implication, no other!] will save his people from their sins" (Matthew 1:21). This is the judgment already registered in heaven concerning Jesus. God has also said, "Whoever believes in the Son has eternal life; whoever does not obey the Son shall not see life, but the wrath of God remains on him" (John 3:36). This is the judgment of heaven concerning Jesus and faith in Jesus: you must believe in the Son if you would have life. Peter, in preaching the gospel, binds and looses in perfect accord with this judgment in heaven.

Perhaps this line of thought sounds strange to you, so listen to the beautiful way John Calvin expresses it: "The substance of this statement [in Matthew 16:19] is, that Christ intended to assure his followers of the salvation promised to them in the Gospel, that they might expect it as firmly as if he were himself to descend from heaven to bear testimony concerning it."[7] Jesus is saying here, "Peter, when you preach the gospel message, as that message in itself opens the kingdom to believers and closes it against unbelievers, God himself is speaking from heaven. When you say to men, 'Believe in Jesus Christ and you shall be saved,' God is speaking." It is not just that in this message, faithfully preached, God himself tells unbelievers there is no other way into the kingdom, and that if they will not come by this way they will not be saved; also in this message, faithfully preached, God tells his believing people that those who trust in his Son will be saved. God himself is speaking these things to us! God himself has come down, as it were, and is preaching in Peter's preaching, so that Peter's binding and loosing is the binding and loosing of God. And on *this Peter*, not Peter the pope (Rome has stretched this text utterly out of proportion; there is nothing here about Peter as a pope), on Peter as confessor and herald of the true gospel, Jesus will build the edifice of his church.

Now look at Matthew 18:15 and notice that the same task of binding and loosing with the keys of the kingdom is later extended to the *whole church* in its discipline. Most of us are familiar with Matthew 18:15–17, "If your brother sins against you, go and tell him his fault, between you and him alone. If he listens to you, you have gained your brother. But if he does not listen, take one or two others along with you . . . . If he refuses to listen to them, tell it to the church. And if he refuses to listen even to the church, let him be to you as a Gentile and a tax collector [*let him be as one who is not even in the kingdom*]." Then in Matthew 18:18, Jesus speaks to the whole church: "Truly, I say to you, whatever you [collectively as the church] bind on earth shall be bound in heaven, and whatever you [collectively] loose on earth shall be loosed in heaven." We see that the church, not just in preaching the gospel but also in its discipline, is exercising the God-given power of binding and loosing.

Put concretely, if there is one in our midst who begins to sin, and someone goes and talks to him or her about the sin, but the response is one of deafness to admonition; then two or three go, meeting the same response; and then the church speaks to that brother or sister, but there is still an obstinate refusal to hear – the person looks the church in the eye and says, "I know what God says, and I'm not going to do it" – we are to regard such a person as having come into the kingdom through some door other than Jesus, and he or she is to be thrown out of the kingdom. Because if you really understand what it is to be reconciled to God through Jesus Christ, if you really understand that your warfare with God has been put to rest through Jesus' death and resurrection, a sure mark that you really understand your reconciliation to God, the Father, the King of heaven and earth, is that you *want to do his will*. Certainly, true believers often struggle with the will of God. We don't always know how to do the will of God. Sometimes we have to fight with ourselves to do the will of God. But in the heart of everyone who really understands, by the working of the Holy Spirit, what Jesus has done in opening the kingdom, there is a fundamental desire to do the will of God. If the church finds in dealing with a brother or sister that this desire is not present, the church is to throw that person out of the kingdom, because he or she has not come in through Jesus. And in this judgment of the church, God himself is registering his judgment as well.

Finally, look at Matthew 28:19–20, and observe how the task first given to Peter, then extended to the whole church in its discipline, is set forth with even greater specificity at the end of Matthew's Gospel when the King comes to his apostles and commands them with "all authority" to go and disciple the nations. He says, in effect, "You are to go out and loose the nations by your preaching of the gospel, opening the door to all who come by faith, shutting it against all who reject the Christ. You are to admit them visibly and officially into the kingdom by baptism. And you are to teach them to observe all that I have revealed to you, all that I have commanded you." In and through this whole task of discipling the nations – preaching, baptizing, teaching, administering the Lord's Supper (one of the Lord's commands, see 1 Corinthians 11:23) – Christ will not only build his church but also the kingdom of God will take visible form.

What is very obvious as you look at the end of verse 20 is that these apostles did not live "to the end of the age." Peter is not still with us. John is not still with us. They died long before the end of the age. What is more, they didn't disciple "all nations." They made some real headway during their lives; and when they died, the task given by Jesus first to Peter and then to the whole church and then to the apostles as a whole in Matthew 28 passed into the hands of pastors, teachers, and overseers in the church (what the Bible calls "elders" or "presbyters"), men officially appointed in the church to preach the Word of God, administer the sacraments, and administer discipline (see Ephesians 4:7–16).

Perhaps by now some of you are thinking, "So what?" This is a valid question, but I hope you can see that everything we have been exploring so far speaks pointedly to the way you and I regard the official administration of Word, sacraments, and discipline in the church. Our King has ordained the preaching and teaching of the Word, the administration of baptism and the Lord's Supper, and the discipline (confrontation, encouragement, and at times even judicial process) of the church. He has ordained these things, not only to loose his people, but also to nourish his people, because he loves his people. The King wants to feed us on his love and grace and truth, and he wants to do so every week. He wants to teach us; he commands the apostles and then the elders of his church to teach his people how to live as free children of God, no longer slaves of Satan, but free children of God. All of this glorious work is committed to the officers of his church.

We must, therefore, ask ourselves pointedly, what is our attitude toward the ordinances of Jesus Christ in the kingdom expression called our local church? Let me be very specific. When the elders of your local church call a worship service, morning or evening, in the name of Christ, when they call a worship service on the Lord's appointed day of worship, the *King* is calling you to worship, and it is *disobedience* not to come. Do you realize that? Your local church is not a spa. It is not a medical clinic. You have no right to decide not to come when the King calls you to worship through his elders. Perhaps you say this sounds heavy-handed. No! The King loves you enough not to let you drift away from these ordinances where alone you can be fed. Many of us have had the experience of being away from worship, through God's providence, for a period of time. Do you not feel your soul beginning to shrivel? Is it not good to come back to the house of the Lord and be fed once again?

As a further application, when the elders of Christ's church administer the Word of God in their official capacity by instructing you, admonishing you, or rebuking you, the *King* is at work. When the elders administer the sacraments, the *King* is at work. When they baptize you, the King is coming to you and setting his name officially and publicly upon you. Your pastor didn't just dream up the idea of baptism; it is Christ's ordinance in the church, so that you may know to the end of your days that you belong to the Father and the Son and the Holy Spirit – you belong to the Triune God, and he loves you everlastingly. And when the elders administer the Lord's Supper, your King himself feeds you, so that you may again and again be told personally and individually, "I have died for you!" He wills that we *feast* on this blessed truth.

The church is not a voluntary society. It is the sphere in which God's loving, gracious, faithful rule of his people concretely operates through the keys of the Word and sacraments and discipline. I say it again: an indicator of how seriously you take the rule of God in your life is how diligently you bring yourself under the ordinances of the church of Jesus Christ, particularly in his gathered worship on his appointed day. *Do not say you love the kingdom* if you will not bring yourself under the King's ordinances. The King's rule is visible in the ordinances of his church. But now to our second point.

THE KING'S RULE IS VISIBLE IN THE OBEDIENCE OF HIS CHURCH

I want to focus here on a little phrase at the beginning of Matthew 28:20, "teaching them to observe [keep, obey] all that I have commanded you." Jesus' kingly authority, he tells us here, will be manifested, it will take visible form on earth, in his disciples' obedience to everything he has commanded. There is a lot in the Gospels that Jesus commanded. He taught us how rightly to apply the Old Testament law; he gave us certain precepts of his own; other of his commands the apostles wrote later in their epistles. But what I want you to notice at present is simply this: *King Jesus has commandments for your life*. Do you realize that? He has a moral will for you to follow; and if you have been admitted to the kingdom by baptism, you are *duty bound* to know that will and to obey that will.

I wonder if perhaps this sounds repulsive to you. I remember wrestling as a younger man with the whole "problem" of authority. I have concluded over the course of my life that I do have a problem with authority. I don't like submission. I don't like someone telling me what to do; and it frightens me sometimes to think about Jesus telling me what to do, because I imagine a gigantic code of laws – like the IRS code – that I must somehow figure out and put into practice, and it sounds as if I'm going to be shriveled and stifled. Do you ever think like this? If we think this way, it shows how little we really understand the commandments of Jesus. Far from shriveling and stifling life, Jesus' commands are the portal to the rich, full, blessed life for which you and I were created. The law of Jesus is an expression to us of the loving, renovating grace of our God. His commandments really reduce to two.

He says to us in Matthew 22:37 and other places that the first and great commandment is to love the Lord your God with all your heart, with all your mind, with all your soul, with all your strength. Think about this first commandment. I said God is *renovating* us, bringing us back into that life for which we were created. How did Adam love his God? He certainly loved God by communing with him at his appointed times. That was one way of loving God, and Adam loved to do it. Adam loved God by speaking God's name always with reverence. I am sure Adam in the garden never, ever said, "Oh my God," in the flippant way some of you do, because he loved this God, and he knew who this God was. Adam would also have loved God by admiring and enjoying God's image in Eve; his relationship with his wife would have been a theater in which he acted out his great love for the God who made her and who made them one flesh.

But – have you thought of this? – Adam would also have loved God just by being a great gardener! I get excited thinking about this. As Adam went out into Eden every day and tended the garden and cultivated it, he was putting on display in his work the same enthusiasm, diligence, and creativity with which the Creator himself engages creation. Adam put on display, as the "lord" of Eden, the glory of how God loves and tends and engages his creation. More than this, Adam also showed the glory of God, and his love for God, by displaying in his work ethic how one made in the image of God works when he is under the smile of God. Adam enjoyed gardening because God was smiling upon him, and the way he gardened reflected the joy of his heart in the joy of God.

We must see that loving God as Jesus commanded does not mean retreating from any sphere of human life and endeavor. It means rather that we bring the glory of God *into* every sphere of human life. In every part of human life, we learn how to display God by our thankfulness to him, by rejoicing in his gifts, by our delight in him, by being able to say when we do this or that that we "feel his pleasure," by our righteousness in playing by the rules (for example, in the sphere of athletics). We bring the goodness and equity of God into these spheres, and thus show forth in them his glory. As redeemed people of God, we have *a reason to do everything!* We have a reason for business, economics, art, athletics, education, artisanship, science, medicine, law, politics, sex, family life, charitable giving, and charitable service. Why? Because for us who love God, every one of these spheres of human life is a theater for serving him and delighting in him. Could anything be *less* restrictive? Could anything be less stifling?

The second command of Jesus you know well. He says it is "like the first." It is to love your neighbor as you love yourself. Our King inaugurated his kingdom – by doing what? By dying for others. You and I show his rule in our lives as we, walking in his footsteps, constantly suffer loss for the sake of others. I can't wear that article of clothing, or I can't take that article of clothing off, because it will cause my neighbor to stumble. I can't speak or write that word, because it will not edify. I can't take this hour to relax, because my neighbor needs me.

I can't eat that food, because it is time to spread a table for the hungry. I can't watch that TV show, because my parents said no. I can't send this email right now, because it is my employer's time.

Yet in "losing" our life in these ways, do we not find it? For in preserving the honor of my neighbor, the life of my neighbor, the chastity of my neighbor, the goods of my neighbor, the reputation of my neighbor, I am actively building the kingdom of *peace*, that kingdom that restores goodwill and harmony and safety and order among humankind. Only those who are obeying Jesus can build this kingdom.

The King engages us in his church in a lifelong mission of reforming life as it was meant to be, as it was created to be – in every sphere of life, in every relationship. We can sometimes begin to think that in the gospel Jesus doesn't demand very much of us. In this we are profoundly mistaken; but he does give us all grace to do all that he commands.

Dietrich Bonhoeffer writes this in the introduction to his book, *The Cost of Discipleship*:

> When the Bible speaks of following Jesus, it is proclaiming a discipleship which will liberate mankind from all man-made dogmas, from every burden and oppression, from every anxiety and torture which afflicts the conscience. If they follow Jesus, men escape from the hard yoke of their own laws, and submit to the kindly yoke of Jesus Christ. But does this mean that we ignore the seriousness of his commands? Far from it. We can only achieve perfect liberty and enjoy fellowship with Jesus when his command, his call to absolute discipleship, is appreciated in its entirety. Only the man who follows this command of Jesus single-mindedly, and unresistingly lets his yoke rest upon him, finds his burden easy, and under its gentle pressure receives the power to persevere in the right way. The command of Jesus is hard, unutterably hard, for those who try to resist it. But for those who willingly submit, the yoke is easy, and the burden is light. . . . His commandment never seeks to destroy life, but to foster, strengthen and heal it.[8]

CONCLUSION

In our final study, we will see that the church's obedience moves in yet another direction as well. We will see that, as Jesus builds his church and restores human life in his church, she is called to go out and bring others into that restored life, and the gates of hell will not prevail against her in that divine mission.

CHAPTER FOUR

THE KINGDOM
AND THE WORLD

Scripture Readings:

Isaiah 2:1–5

1 Corinthians 15:23–28

Acts 1:6–8

INTRODUCTION

In June of 1914, at the Princeton Summer School of Theology, Dr. Benjamin B. Warfield delivered five lectures that we now know by their published title, *The Plan of Salvation*. The purpose of these five lectures was, in Warfield's words, to show that "God deals throughout the whole process of salvation not with men in the mass but with individual men one by one, upon each of whom he lays hold with his grace, and each of whom he by his grace brings to salvation."[9] Warfield was defending in his lectures the precious truth that God saves his people *particularly*. He doesn't just save a mass of people (true though that is), he saves individuals; by irresistible grace, he saves particular men and women, boys and girls. It was *particularism* that Warfield was concerned to expound.

Now, given this explicit purpose of the lectures, it is really quite startling when in the fifth and final lecture we run across the following remarkable passage:

> The redemption of Christ, if it is to be worthily viewed, must be looked at not merely individualistically, but also in its social, or better in its cosmical relations. Men are not discrete particles standing off from one another as mutually isolated units. They are members of an organism, the human race; and this race itself is an element in a greater organism which is significantly termed a universe. Of course the plan of salvation as it lies in the divine mind cannot be supposed to be concerned, therefore, alone with individuals as such: it of necessity has its relations with the greater unities into which these individuals enter as elements. We have only partially understood the redemption in Christ, therefore, when we have thought of it only in its modes of operation and effects on the individual. We must ask also how and what it works in the organism of the human race, and what its effects are in the greater organism of the universe. Jesus Christ came to save men, but he did not come to save men each as a whole in himself out of relation to all other men. In saving men, he came to save mankind; and therefore the Scriptures are insistent that he came to save the world, and ascribe to him

accordingly the great title of the Saviour of the world. They go indeed further than this: they do not pause in expanding their outlook until they proclaim that it was the good pleasure of God "to sum up all things in Christ, the things in the heavens, and the things on the earth." We have not done justice to the Biblical doctrine of the plan of salvation therefore so long as we confine our attention to the modes of the divine operation in saving the individual, and insist accordingly on what we have called its particularism. There is a wider prospect on which we must feast our eyes if we are to view the whole land of salvation. It was because God loved the world, that he sent his only-begotten Son; it was for the sins of the world that Jesus Christ made propitiation; it was the world which he came to save; it is nothing less than the world that shall be saved by him.[10]

Warfield, as those of you who have read him will know, was not a man given to theological excesses. He was not some sort of eschatological dreamer, like certain writers of our own time. He was a man of acute theological insight and precision; and yet he writes this passage, which to the ears of his fellow Calvinists is almost shocking. Why? Why would Warfield, in the midst of lectures devoted to the idea that God saves individuals particularly, sound such a *universalistic* note? To answer this question I want to situate what Warfield says in the context of our four studies on the kingdom of God.

Since we first heard Jesus announce in Mark 1:14–15 that "the time has been fulfilled" and the kingdom of God has now arrived, we have been learning that the substance of the glad tidings that define us as Christians, the substance of what we call the "gospel," is the kingdom of God come to earth. The *cornerstone* of this kingdom, we have also learned, is the death of the King. A strange cornerstone for a kingdom, to be sure, but there it is. The King dies, and in his death, which God accepts on behalf of his people, the King crushes Satan. He shatters all the power structures of Satan's kingdom, because in his death he has fully borne and absorbed in himself God's curse upon our sin, and as a result our destroyer and accuser cannot accuse and destroy us anymore; we are liberated from his bondage. The apostle Paul says God has translated us out of the kingdom of darkness into the kingdom of the Son of his love, "in whom we have redemption, the forgiveness of sins" (Colossians 1:13–14). A new, *uncursed* humanity has been born. Christ the great King, in his death on the cross, stripped Satan of all power over this new humanity, of which he himself is the Firstborn and Head.

We have also learned that the invisible victory of King Jesus (no one physically saw Satan thrown down in the events of the cross and resurrection) takes *visible form* in the earth. The invisible victory of Jesus produces visible effects in time and history. It takes visible form (recall from our last study) in the ordinances and obedience of the church; but now I want to show you that it also takes visible form, it also produces visible effects, in the *world as a whole*.

This may sound a bit strange to you. I believe many Christians, including many Reformed Christians, think as follows about the salvation of God in the world: Many of us view the world as a burning building. Jesus, praise his grace, has given us an escape ladder; and the great goal of the Christian life is to dash about the burning building, giving people the good news that there is an escape ladder out of the building. This is how we think about salvation: God is snatching individuals out of the burning building of the world, giving them an escape ladder by which they may mercifully escape.

Let me say to you boldly: I believe this way of thinking is not only erroneous; there is a sense in which it is abominable. A better metaphor, whatever its weaknesses, would be that we are living in a very dilapidated building – dilapidated, because it is full of dead people. The building is owned by God himself, but a parasitic landlord has come in and slain the inhabitants, and the building has begun to rot. The Owner, however, has gloriously reentered his building and has actually raised some of its inhabitants from the dead. He has given to these quickened inhabitants his own life-giving Word, and commissioned them to go and preach that Word to other dead inhabitants of the building, that they, too, by the power of the Owner, may be raised to new life.

This is not all he has given to us, though. He has not just given us his Word that raises inhabitants of the building from the dead; he has also given us the blueprints for the restoration of the building, and he has told us to build and restore in this building until he comes again fully to restore it. With all its weaknesses, this is a far better metaphor. There is *renovative work* to be done in the "building" of this world before the Owner returns.

This may seem to you, again, a somewhat controversial suggestion; and it may not be obvious to you just how it works out in real life. There is a massive set of ideas bound up in what I am trying to say. Our work in this study can be little more than suggestive, but hopefully it will also be provocative and edifying. I want to unpack two main ideas in this study, using the two texts we have read in 1 Corinthians and in Acts. First, we will spend a few moments reflecting on the reign of Christ and the history of the world.

THE REIGN OF CHRIST AND THE HISTORY OF THE WORLD

How does the invisible reign of Christ take visible form – what are its visible effects – in the history of the world? This question ushers us into the flow of Paul's thinking in our first text, 1 Corinthians 15:23–28. We need to try to see the basic structure of what Paul is doing as we begin in verse 23.

Paul sets forth in verse 23 two "orders" of resurrection. Christ is the "firstfruits"; that day 2000 years ago when God by the Holy Spirit raised Jesus from the dead was the firstfruits, the first order, of resurrection. The second order of resurrection is identified with those who belong to Jesus, whom he will raise up at the last day when he returns. "Christ the firstfruits, then at his coming those who belong to Christ." Now, you will notice that Paul almost collapses these two orders together in verse 23. In a sense, they are simply two parts of one great resurrection event; they are not so much two resurrections as *one* resurrection that comes in two parts. Christ is the firstfruits. The firstfruits are part of the whole harvest, and the whole harvest will come in that second order of the resurrection event at the last day.

But what does Paul tell us is going on *between* the two orders of resurrection? He says that what is going on between the two orders is the *kingdom*. Note what he says in verse 27, "God has put all things in subjection under [Jesus'] feet." When did this occur? Paul leaves no ambiguity in his Ephesians epistle: "[God] raised [Jesus] from the dead and seated him at his right hand in the heavenly places, far above all rule and authority and power and dominion, and above every name that is named" (Ephesians 1:20–21). God put all things in subjection under Jesus' feet when he raised him from the dead and seated him at his right hand; this is precisely what Paul is referring to here in verse 27. In Jesus' resurrection, ascension, and "session" at the right hand of the Father, God the Father put all things under his feet; the reign of Christ began when he sat down at the right hand of the Father.

Now notice what Paul tells us in verse 26 about the consummation, the "other end" of Christ's kingdom. The "last enemy" Christ the King will destroy is death. In the last great battle of his kingdom, the King will crush death in all of its manifestations; he will take away not only the death that has come upon the souls of his people but also the death that affects our bodies. *In between those two poles* – the resurrection/ascension/session of Jesus, and his raising us up from the dead at the last day – is what Paul calls "the kingdom" (verse 24).

We can now ask another question: What will go on during this kingdom period? What sorts of things will occur in this period? Paul's answer is that Jesus "must reign [as King] until he has put all his enemies under his feet" (verse 25). This seems to indicate that Jesus' activity of subduing his enemies, of putting them visibly under his feet, is something that goes on *throughout the whole period of his reign*, from his ascension to the Father's right hand until the last battle with the enemy called death. Admittedly, this is not perfectly clear from verse 25, but it is considerably clearer in verse 24: Paul, speaking about the very end of all things (the second order of resurrection), says Jesus will deliver his kingdom to the Father "after destroying" or "when he has put an end to" all his enemies, "every rule and every authority and power." Note the sequence. It is even more explicit in verse 28. Paul works through the same sequence again: "When all things are [or have been] subjected to him [Jesus], *then the Son himself will also be subjected* to [the Father] who put all things in subjection under him, that God may be all in all."

What this sequence – sitting at the right hand of the Father; then putting his enemies under his feet; then, when all things have been subjected to him, delivering the kingdom up to the Father – what this sequence tells us, is that you and I are living in the period in which Christ is putting an end to all rule and all power and all authority that opposes him, whether in heaven or here on earth. *He is doing this now.* It is a work that will not be completed until the last day, certainly; but he is doing it now, and surely such a work must take *some visible form.*

We can demonstrate this quite simply if we reflect on our individual lives. We expect to see *visible* – admittedly gradual, but visible – progress of Christ's life-giving, liberating rule in our individual lives, do we not? Isn't this what we mean when we speak of "progressive sanctification"? Thank Jesus, he doesn't save me one day and then leave me to muddle about in my sins the rest of my life. When Jesus becomes my King, he takes over: he starts smashing down walls, walking into closets where I haven't invited him, taking things out of my drawers, and claiming ownership over everything I have and everything I am – and I expect to see Jesus' reign in my individual life take visible form as he throws down in me "arguments and every lofty opinion raised against the knowledge of God" (2 Corinthians 10:4–5).

We expect the same thing in our family lives. I believe with all my heart I will be a better father and husband in ten years than I am today, because my King is throwing down everything that opposes him in my family life. I also expect to see my wife more sanctified and my children more sanctified as time goes on. The invisible rule of Jesus takes visible form in my soul, in my personal life, and in my family life.

We expect to see this in the church. I expect to see in my generation the frontiers of missions pushed farther than they have been already – and surely we have come a very long way from those early days of the mission in Jerusalem and Judea, have we not? The kingdom of Christ is going out, it is taking visible form in and through the church, it is expanding throughout the world. Why, then, would we not expect to see similar visible victories for our Lord in the world – for example, in subduing kings and political rulers and political power structures?

Perhaps you ask, "What are you talking about?" Is it too much to think that, perhaps even in our own generation, we might see *Roe v. Wade* reversed; not because of some ridiculous Darwinian notion that we need to preserve the species, but because the High King of heaven and earth has said it is wickedness to slay our offspring? Might we expect to see our legislatures reject civil unions of homosexual couples; not, again, because of mere tradition or sociological evidence that children are happier in a heterosexual couple's home, but because the God and King of the universe has defined marriage, and we have no right to tamper with his definition? Might we expect to see governments stop stealing from their people; not because it is better for the economy, but because Christ the King has ordained laws to govern kings and political rulers for the good of their people? Should we not expect to see some visible victories for our Lord in these arenas? Or what about our educational institutions? Might we not expect – do we not have a right to expect – that we will see the God-given rights and responsibilities of parents fully acknowledged by our educational institutions? What about our cultural forms? Might we see in our own time blasphemous and pornographic art suppressed in our society? Should we not pray for this and seek this? Do we have no right to pray for these things? These are ways in which the invisible rule of Jesus the King takes visible form; these are ways in which he *visibly* throws down rule and power and authority that oppose him in heaven and on earth, because *all things*, says Paul, without exception – all spheres of human life – are under his feet. He is the Lord of the state as much as of the church. He is the Lord of education and culture. He is the King over all things. Maybe you are saying to yourself, "This sounds far too sociopolitical!" My friend, the gospel *is* sociopolitical! The gospel is the *kingdom*. The gospel is about the universal, life-restoring rule of Jesus Christ. It is inherently sociopolitical.

But now let us turn from the reign of Christ in the history of the world to the reign of Christ in and through the mission of the church.

THE REIGN OF CHRIST AND THE MISSION OF THE CHURCH

Here we go backward to Acts 1. Paul in 1 Corinthians 15 tells us something about what Jesus is doing in the period of his reign, and gives us reason to expect visible effects, a visible form of that reign in world history. But he leaves open an important question; you are probably already feeling it: Apart from simply acting supernaturally from heaven, *how* does Jesus advance his rule during the period of his reign? *How* does he subdue his enemies prior to his coming again? Paul doesn't have to answer that question in 1 Corinthians 15, because Jesus already answered it in Acts 1!

As the book of Acts opens, Jesus' disciples have been hearing a great deal about the kingdom of God, and now it seems their Lord is about to leave them, and they still haven't seen Caesar overthrown. They haven't seen a lot of the radical things the Jews were expecting from their Messiah, and so they ask Jesus, "Lord, will you at this time restore the kingdom to Israel?" In effect, they are saying, "Lord, we've received all these prophecies over all these centuries about your bringing the kingdom and restoring it to your people. Are you going to do it now, Lord?"

Jesus in a very interesting way adjusts their perspective. He tells them first of all that the issue is not *when* God is going to build his kingdom. It is not for these disciples, nor is it for us today, to know the precise times and seasons God the Father has set for particular manifestations of Christ's kingdom in history, or certainly for the final and grandest manifestation of Christ's kingdom-victory when he returns. We are not to know the times and seasons (verse 7); that is not what we are to be thinking about. We are rather to give our attention to *how* God builds his kingdom. God builds his kingdom, Jesus says in verse 8, through *the Spirit-empowered witness of the church to Jesus Christ*: "You will receive power when the Holy Spirit has come upon you, and you will be my witnesses. Your witness will begin in Jerusalem; it will spread to Judea; it will spread to Samaria; it will spread to the end of the earth. You are to be my witnesses. That is how I will build my kingdom."

The disciples need their perspective corrected in a second area as well. They are still thinking entirely in terms of national Israel. Jesus tells them they need to stop thinking about how he is going to restore the kingdom to Israel and start thinking about how he is going to build his kingdom in the *entire world*, as their Spirit-empowered witness radiates out from Mount Zion in Jerusalem to the ends of the earth. This brings before us the question: What precisely is the church to witness about Jesus Christ? Of what are we to bear witness?

First, the church is to witness of Jesus Christ that *he is the Sin-bearer who brings God's reconciling grace to the world.* That is the first thing we are to tell the world. We are to tell them about the Creator who has a holy law for his creatures, and that humankind has in its entirety rebelled against this law, transgressed it, and refused to obey it. We call this kind of witnessing "personal evangelism." We talk to people in the world and appeal to the witness in their own hearts and consciences that sin is real. People don't have to be Christians to understand sin, because God has impressed a sense of his moral requirements upon their hearts; they know the world is full of evil.

A few months ago at the time of this writing, the movie *Dark Knight* began playing in theaters. It is a profound film, in that it wrestles almost to the point of anguish with the question (framed here from a Christian perspective), "How we are to define and respond to evil in a world that has thrown God's law to the wind?" Viewers are made to feel the effects as a society with no place for God begins to unravel morally. We can use films like this to tell people about the Creator, his law, and human sin. We tell them, too, about the judgment to come. We certainly go on to tell them about the pardon God extends to sinners in the blood of his Son. The blood of the Son has appeased the wrath of God; and in that blood, God reconciles sinners to himself. (Perhaps you struggle to witness this way about Jesus. If so, you can certainly invite people to come and hear preaching. Invite them to church! If your pastor is doing his job, he should be preaching every week about Jesus, the Sin-bearer who brings God's reconciling grace to the world.)

The church has repeatedly been tempted to seek social transformation without bearing witness to the cross and the resurrection, to Jesus as the Sin-bearer and the agent of God's reconciling grace. It has repeatedly been tempted to water down its message, and to seek the moral effects of the gospel without the gospel. The Holy Spirit will never own such a message or such a project, for the Spirit has come to bear witness to him who was crucified and resurrected, and this is where we *must* begin if we would see God's transforming work in our society. The foundation of kingdom transformation is always the message of the death of the King.

That being said, I fear the church has often borne witness to a half-Christ, because we have not testified of a second thing, which is no less essential. Jesus is not only the Sin-bearer who brings God's reconciling grace to the world. He is also *the Lawgiver who brings God's renovating grace to the world.* By his revealed moral will for humankind, Jesus renovates human life back into that glory for which God created it. Recall what he commanded his apostles (paraphrasing from Matthew 28): "Go, and make disciples of the nations, not only telling them about the cross and resurrection, but also teaching them to obey everything I have commanded. I have a law. I have commands." This is what is pictured for us in Isaiah 2. The nations stream uphill to Zion, the "mountain of the house of the Lord," exalted above the mountains, because "out of Zion," they say, "shall go the law, and the word of the Lord from Jerusalem" (Isaiah 2:2–3).

We must understand, not only for our witness to the world, but also for ourselves, that pardon in Christ's blood is never an end in itself. If in our thinking about salvation God's pardoning us has become an end in itself, then we don't understand salvation. God never pardons anyone and leaves it at that. God reconciles us to himself through the blood of Jesus in order that his great purposes in creating human life may be fulfilled. God created humankind for a purpose, and nothing less than the total fulfillment of that purpose will satisfy him.

This means, then, that not only our *souls* are to be brought under the transforming, renovating rule of Jesus; all human callings, all spheres of human life and enterprise are likewise to be brought under his transforming, renovating rule. I do not expect Jesus to sanctify me only in my soul. I expect him to sanctify me in my callings as a father, as a husband, as a citizen, as an employee. We as a church should expect to see the renovating rule of Jesus transforming all of our callings as fathers, mothers, husbands, wives, kings, magistrates, businesspersons, artists, and so on.

What would we do if a national president fell on his face, confessed Jesus as Lord, and said (as a soldier said to John the Baptizer), "What must I do?" We would say to him, "The King of kings has a law for you, too. He will tell you how to discharge your calling as a king, as a president." The same is true for all magistrates and educators and economists and businesspersons and scientists and artists. There is no human calling, there is no sphere of human life, over which Jesus does not intend to extend his transforming, life-giving rule. In every calling, in every sphere of human enterprise, the people of earth are to be taught to put off sin and to put on righteousness and goodness. Every square inch of human life is to be dedicated and conducted to the glory of God. In connection with this, listen to the great Geerhardus Vos:

> The visible church is [not] the only outward expression of the invisible kingdom. Undoubtedly, the kingdom of God, as his recognized and applied supremacy, is intended to pervade and control the whole of human life in all its forms of existence. . . . There is a sphere of science, a sphere of art, a sphere of the family and of the state, a sphere of commerce and industry. Whenever one of these spheres comes under the controlling influence of the principle of the divine supremacy and glory, and this outwardly reveals itself, there we can truly say that the kingdom of God has become manifest.[11]

It may be well to register a clarification at this point. It is certainly not true that Jesus gives detailed precepts, a whole code of legislation, for every one of these spheres of human life. You and I will find, and will help others discover, that the question of how to do all things to God's glory in a fallen world is often more a matter of *wisdom* than of law. Think of this in the sphere of the arts: Suppose a Jimmy Hendrix is converted? Can he still perform "Purple Haze" to the glory of God? If a Michael Mann is converted, can he still produce *Collateral?* What about us? Can believers appreciate a Marcel Duchamp exhibit to the glory of God? These are hard questions, questions on which Christ does not necessarily give us explicit law, but questions that require us to think with great wisdom, seeking to work our way out from Christ's commandments in order to do what is wise, bringing all of life – and this is the point – under what Vos calls "the controlling influence" of God's supremacy, righteousness, beauty, goodness, and truth.

And may I confidently say to you that, as the law of Christ prevails in all of these spheres of human life, as the church disciples the nations, we will see society, culture, and civilization transformed.

In all of these spheres, as surely as in the salvation of individual souls, the gates of hell will not prevail against the witness of the church. Dennis Johnson comments beautifully on our text here in Acts 1:6–8, "Luke highlights the powerful force of God's Spirit, propelling divine vitality, purity and grace out from the ancient holy place to bring the nations under the redemptive rule of the Lord and his Christ."[12]

CONCLUSION

Let me try now to bring all of this to a sharper point. In whatever little outpost of witness you find yourself sitting today – perhaps on the rim of a great city, perhaps in a cornfield, perhaps in a hut on a poverty-stricken mission field – what are you expecting from your King? Do you expect your God to save souls? Do you really *expect* this? Do you expect your King to transform human callings, to renovate commerce, art, government, and home life around you? Do you expect Christ to go out with you and, by the power of his Holy Spirit who bears witness with your witness, really to renovate whole spheres of human life? Do you expect to see such things? Do you believe Jesus will change your neighborhood, your place of work, your city, your nation? Do you pray that the kingdom of God will come, and his will be done on earth as it is in heaven; and do you believe this prayer is being and will be answered? I wonder if you do; I confess that often I do not. It may take generations; but do we expect Christ to make his rule visible in the world around us? Or are we just thankful we're not going to burn with the building? Are we content to retreat into our little Christian ghetto and listen to sermons until Jesus comes?

The book of Acts ends, as you know, in chapter 28. By that time, Paul has invaded Nero's household, and the gospel of the kingdom has penetrated into Rome, the center of the civilized world, into the very household of Caesar. The book of Acts has nothing less than world conquest in view! So should we.

I can think of no better way to close this series of studies on the kingdom of God than with Peter Leithart's marvelous statement about the mission of the church:

The church, as a colaborer with God, is called to nothing less than world conquest, world construction, in the widest possible sense. She is called to labor by God's power to bring every man, woman, and child into the life and under the dominion of the kingdom; to work to see that every institution in every nation conforms itself to Christ's commandments; to bring every thought into captivity to Christ (2 Cor. 10:5). Her mission is to see that every human being brings every created thing into service to God . . . . [The] Church has a *mission*, and what a mission![13]

ENDNOTES

PREFACE

[1] Abraham Kuyper, *Calvinism* (Grand Rapids: William B. Eerdmans, 1943), 79 (emphasis in original).

CHAPTER ONE: THE KINGDOM AND THE COVENANT

[2] Herman Bavinck, *Prolegomena*, vol. 1 of *Reformed Dogmatics*, ed. John Bolt, trans. John Vriend (Grand Rapids: Baker Academic, 2003), 112.

[3] Depending on how they are defined, these two phrases are not always interchangeable; but for our purposes they will be used synonymously to refer to the canonical Scriptures of Israel.

[4] If this imagery seems foreign to us, it would have been unthinkable in the agricultural community of Israel to take a grapevine from one's vineyard, where it was needed to bear fruit, and use it as a hitching post for a donkey. But when Shiloh comes, "nature will be renewed so much" that even hitching posts will be fruitful vines! See Stephen G. Dempster, *Dominion and Dynasty: A Theology of the Hebrew Bible*, vol. 15 of *New Studies in Biblical Theology*, ed. D. A. Carson (Nottingham: Apollos; Downers Grove, IL: InterVarsity Press, 2003), 91.

CHAPTER TWO: THE KINGDOM AND THE SINNER

[5] John Owen, *A Practical Exposition upon Psalm CXXX*, vol. VI of *The Works of John Owen*, ed. William H. Goold (Oxford: Johnstone & Hunter, 1850–53; reprint, Edinburgh: Banner of Truth Trust, 1966), 534.

CHAPTER THREE: THE KINGDOM AND THE CHURCH

[6] Geerhardus Vos, "The Kingdom of God," in *Redemptive History and Biblical Interpretation: The Shorter Writings of Geerhardus Vos*, ed. Richard B. Gaffin, Jr. (Phillipsburg, NJ: Presbyterian and Reformed Publishing, 1980), 315.

[7] John Calvin, *Commentary on a Harmony of the Evangelists, Matthew, Mark, and Luke*, trans. William Pringle, vol. XVI of *Calvin's Commentaries* (Edinburgh: Calvin Translation Society; reprint, Grand Rapids: Baker Books, 2003), 294.

[8] Dietrich Bonhoeffer, *The Cost of Discipleship* (New York: Macmillan, 1959; reprint, New York: Touchstone, 1995), 37–38.

CHAPTER FOUR: THE KINGDOM AND THE WORLD

[9] Benjamin B. Warfield, *The Plan of Salvation* (Presbyterian Board of Publication, 1915; reprint, Avinger, TX: Simpson Publishing Co., 1989), 15.

[10] Ibid., 102–3.

[11] Geerhardus Vos, *The Teaching of Jesus Concerning the Kingdom of God and the Church* (Phillipsburg, NJ: Presbyterian and Reformed Publishing Co., 1972), 87–88.

[12] Dennis E. Johnson, *The Message of Acts in the History of Redemption* (Phillipsburg, NJ: Presbyterian and Reformed Publishing Co., 1997), 8.

[13] Peter J. Leithart, *The Kingdom and the Power: Rediscovering the Centrality of the Church* (Phillipsburg, NJ: Presbyterian and Reformed Publishing Co., 1993), 173–74.

www.ingramcontent.com/pod-product-compliance
Lightning Source LLC
Chambersburg PA
CBHW021910040426
42447CB00007B/793